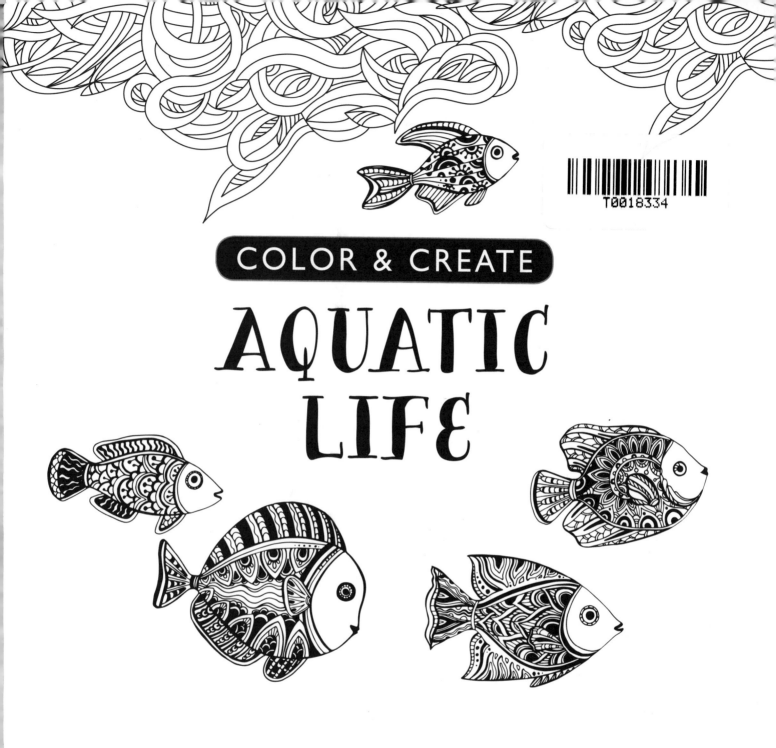

COLOR & CREATE

AQUATIC LIFE

PaRragon

Bath · New York · Cologne · Melbourne · Delhi
Hong Kong · Shenzhen · Singapore

T0018334

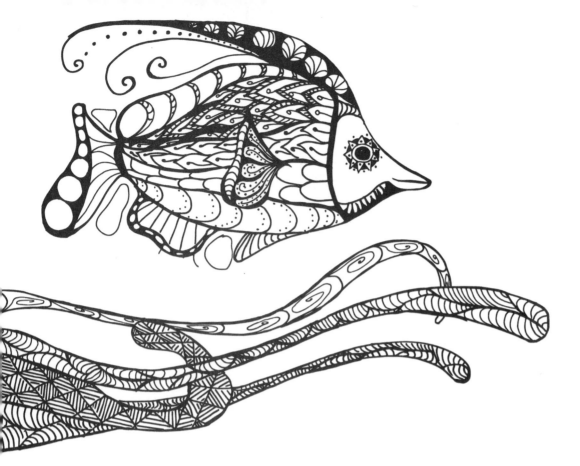

This edition published by Parragon Books Ltd in 2016
and distributed by

Parragon Inc.
440 Park Avenue South, 13th Floor
New York, NY 10016
www.parragon.com

Images are courtesy of Shutterstock and iStock
Cover design by Nigel Partridge

ISBN 978-1-4748-4174-0

Printed in US

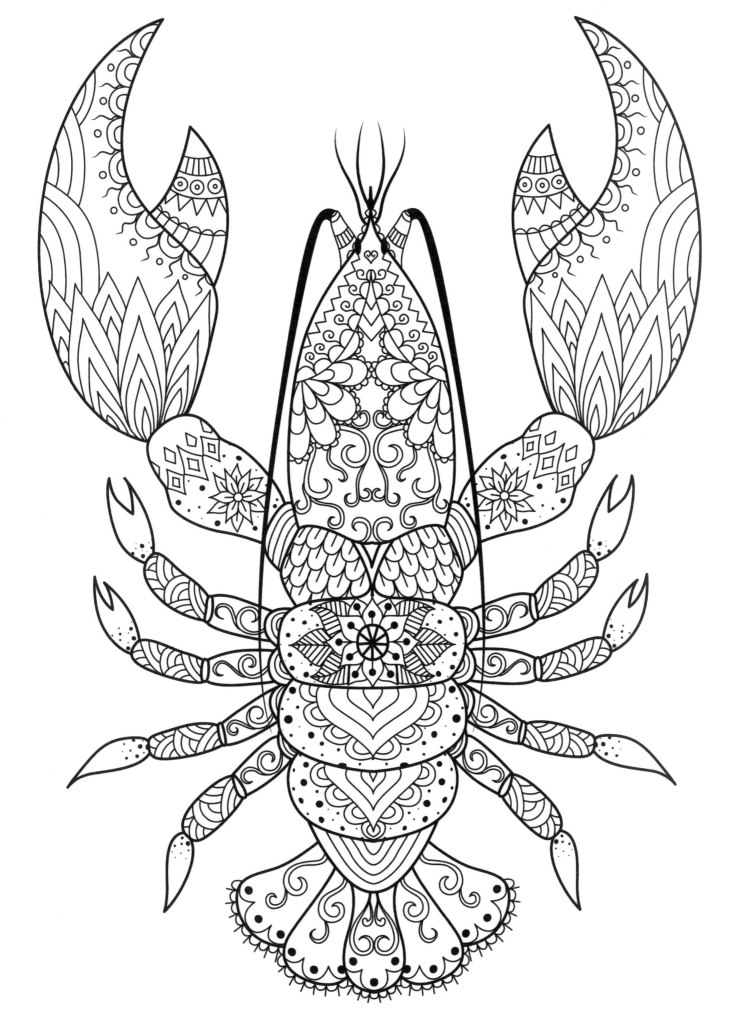

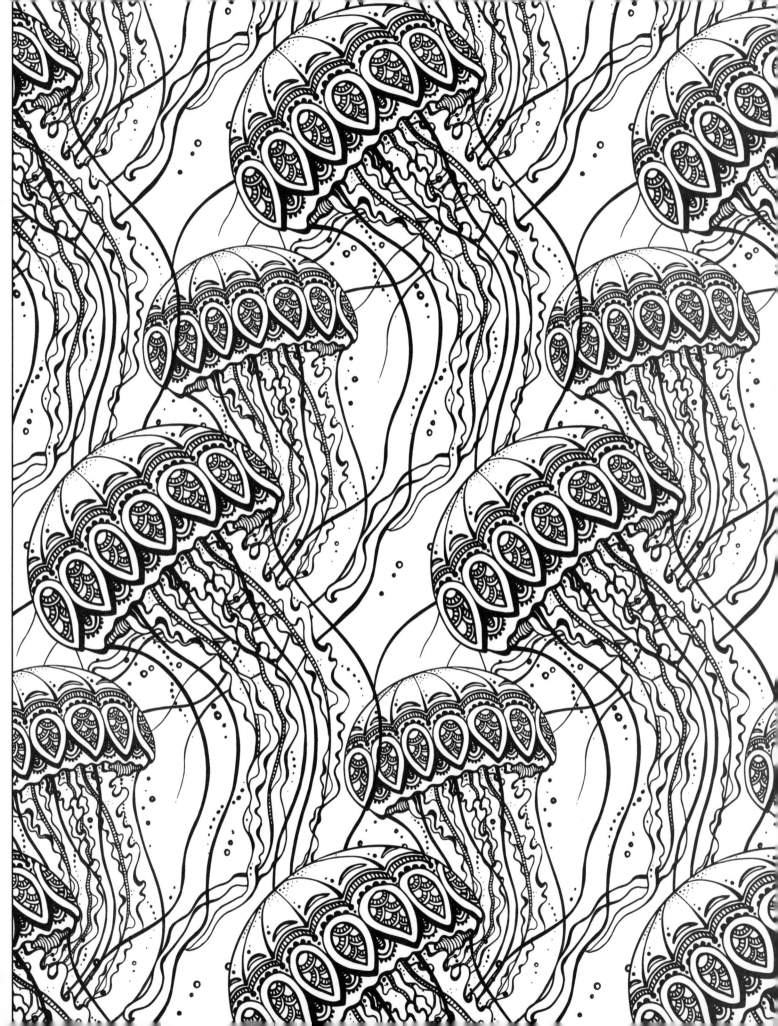

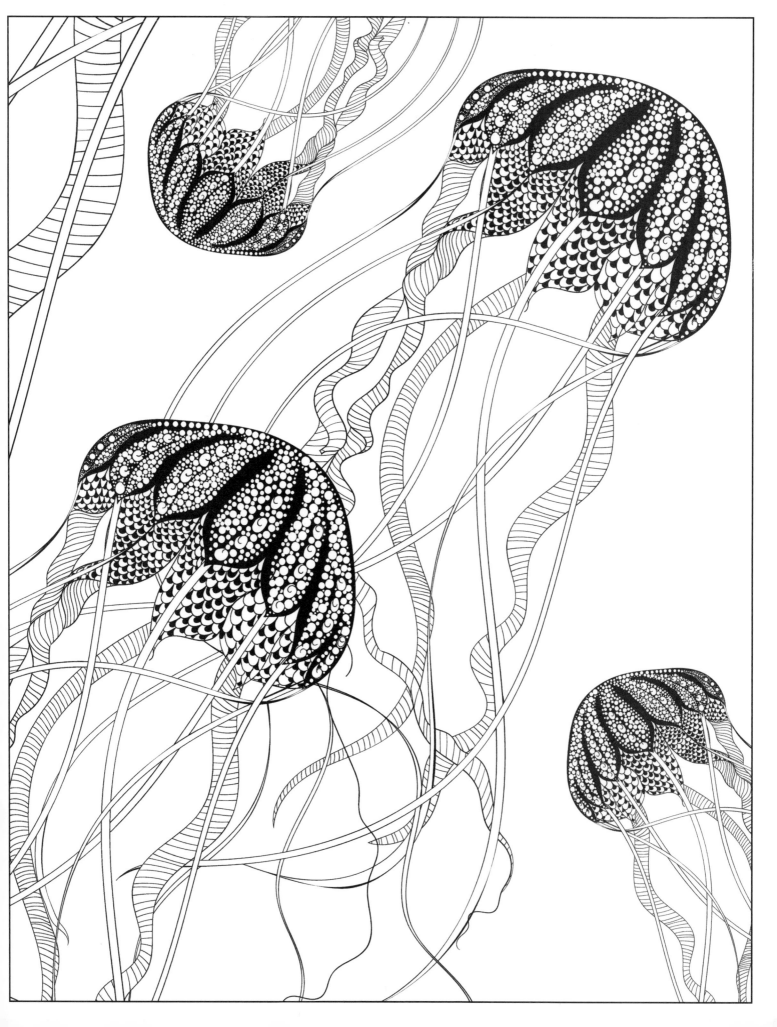

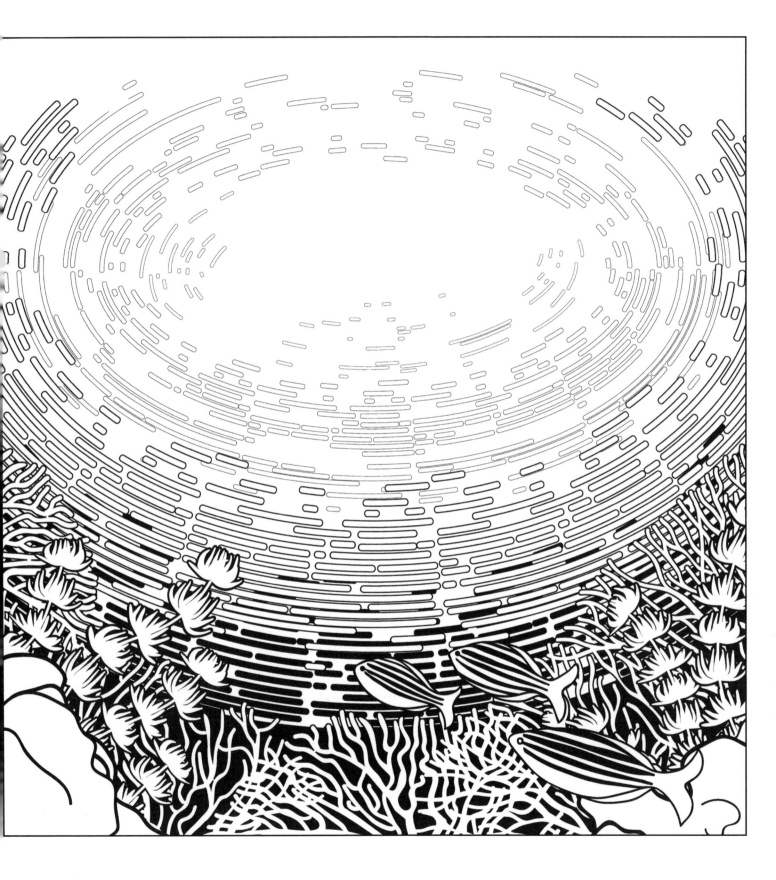

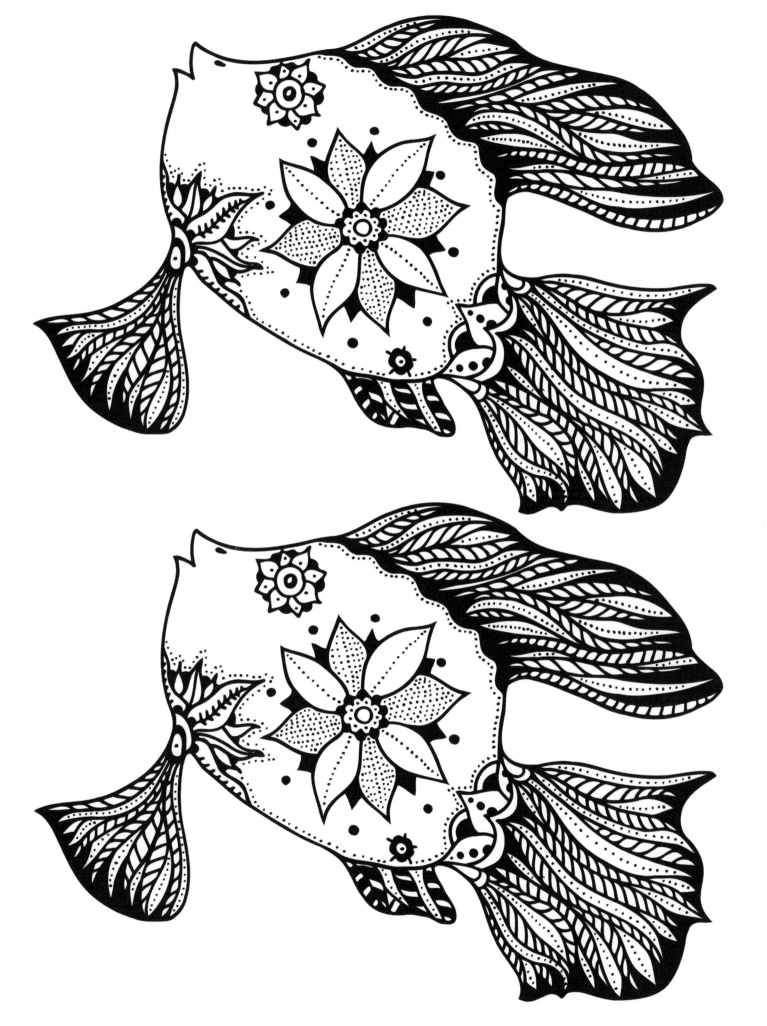

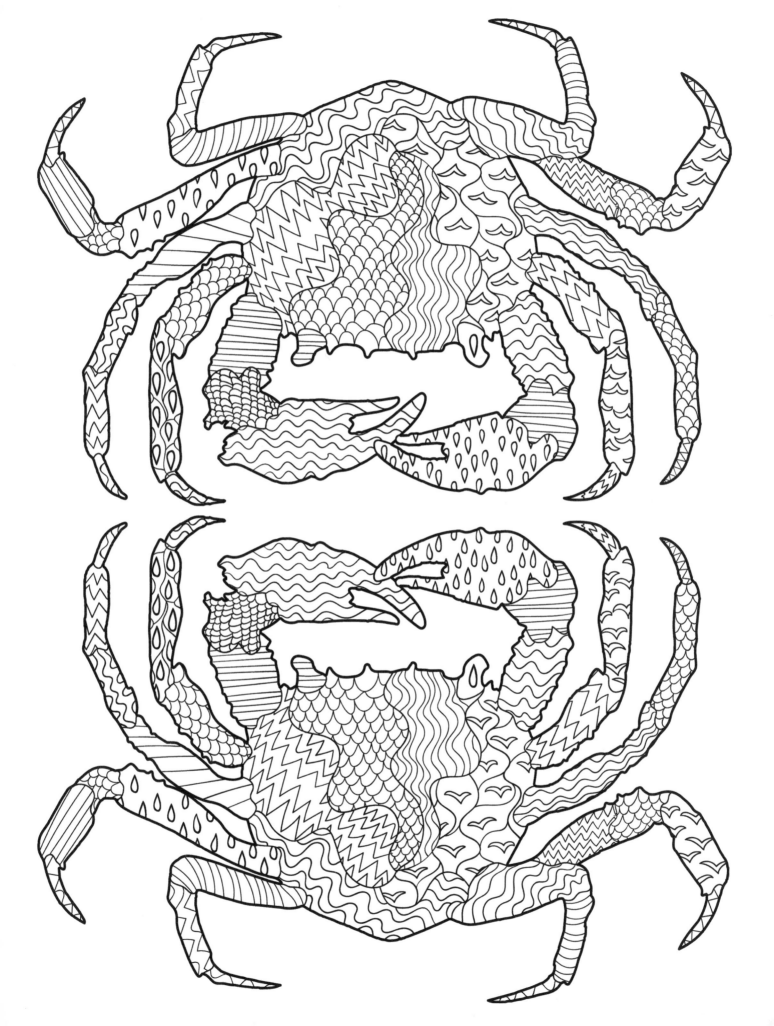

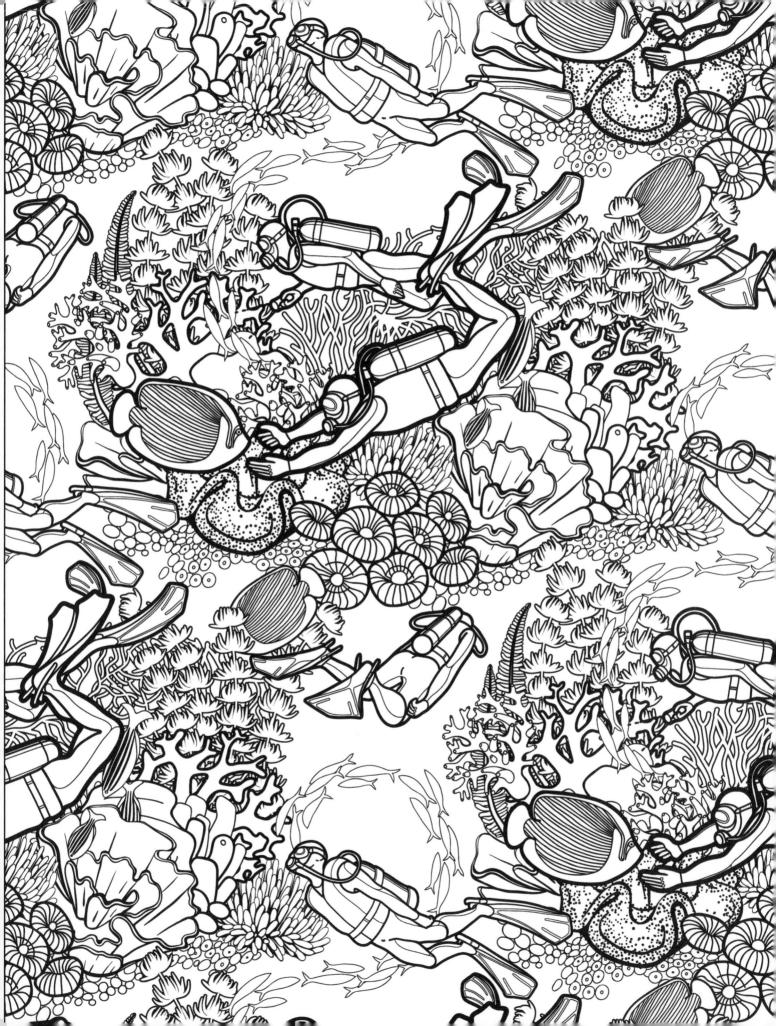

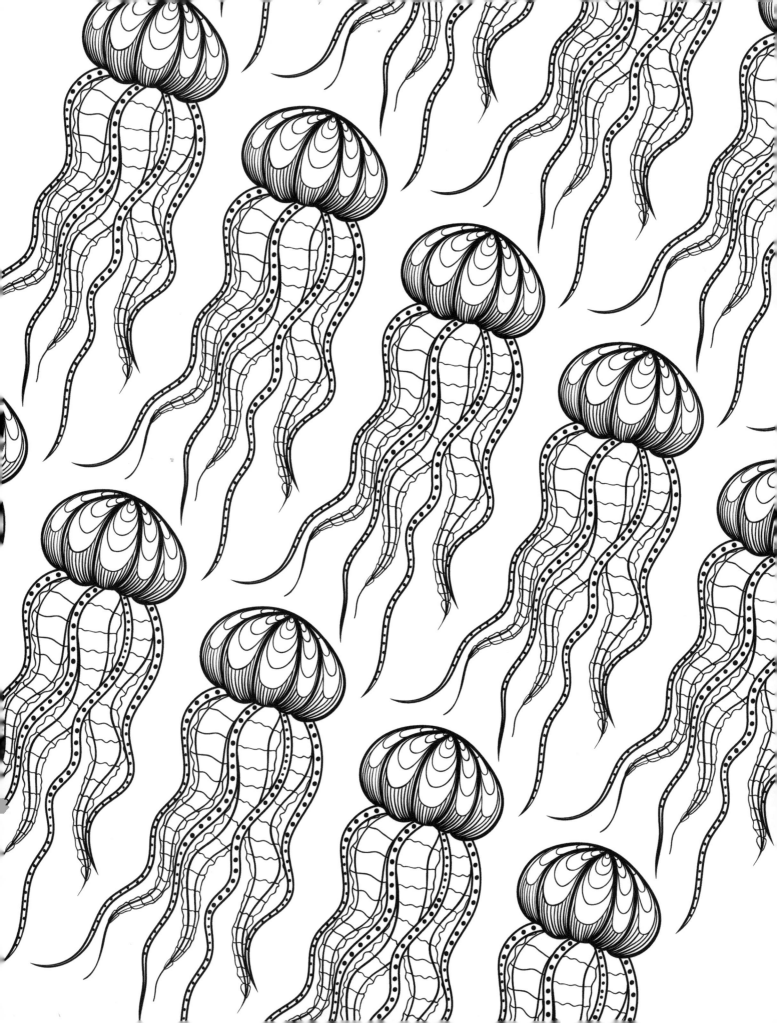

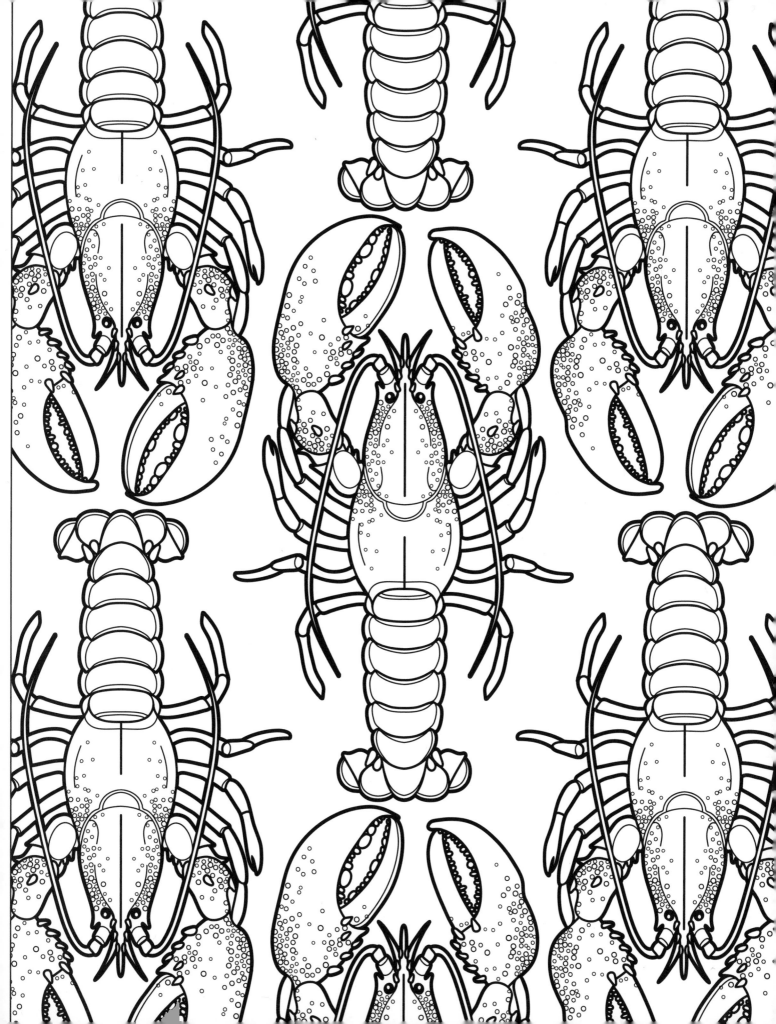

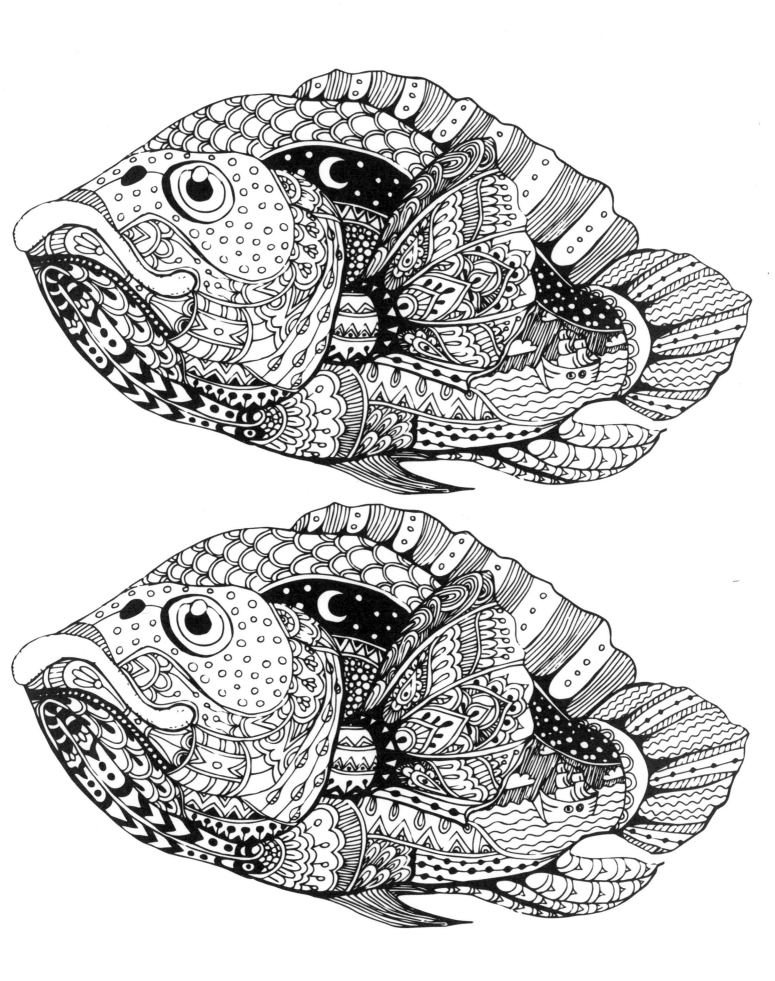

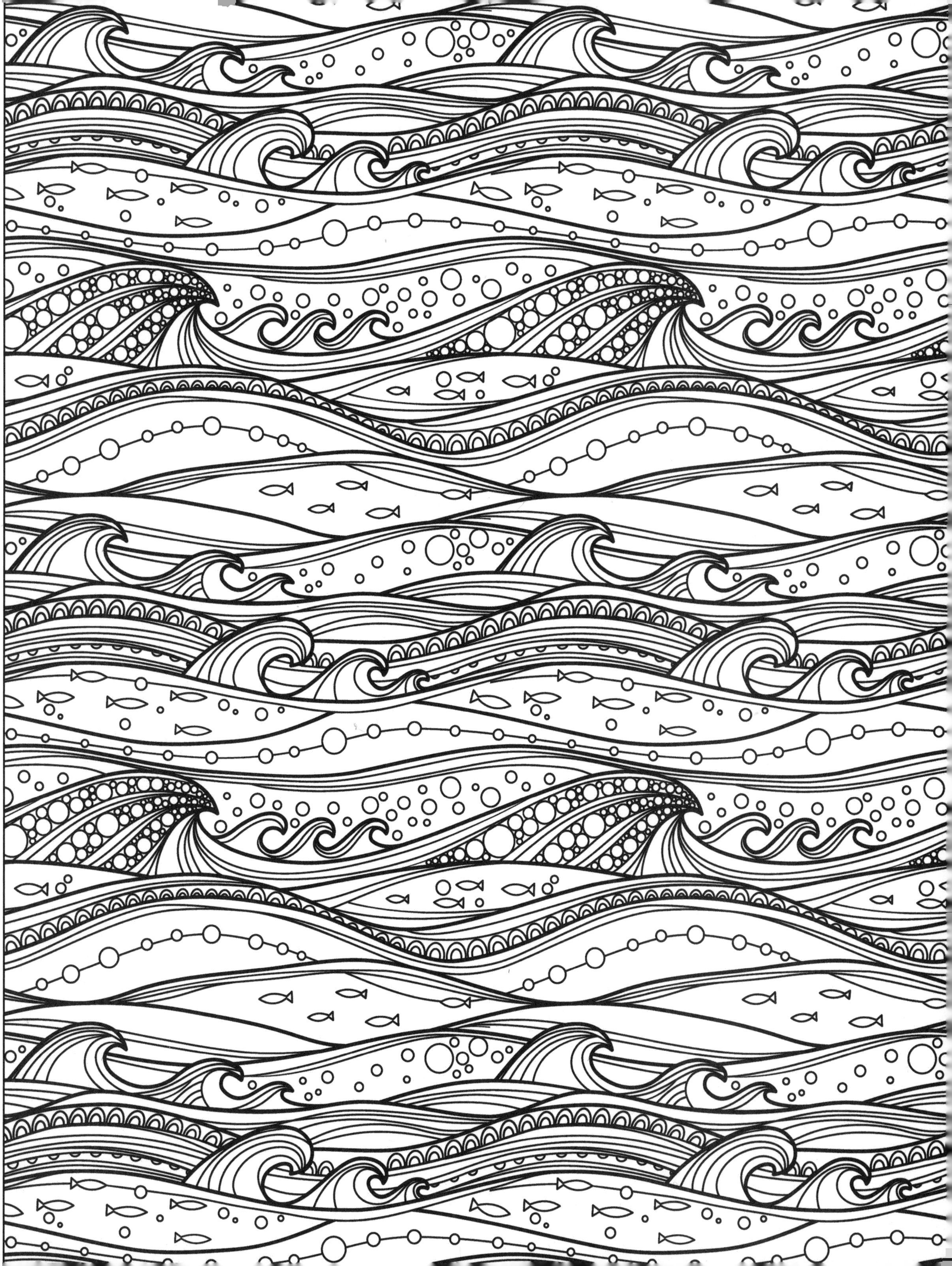

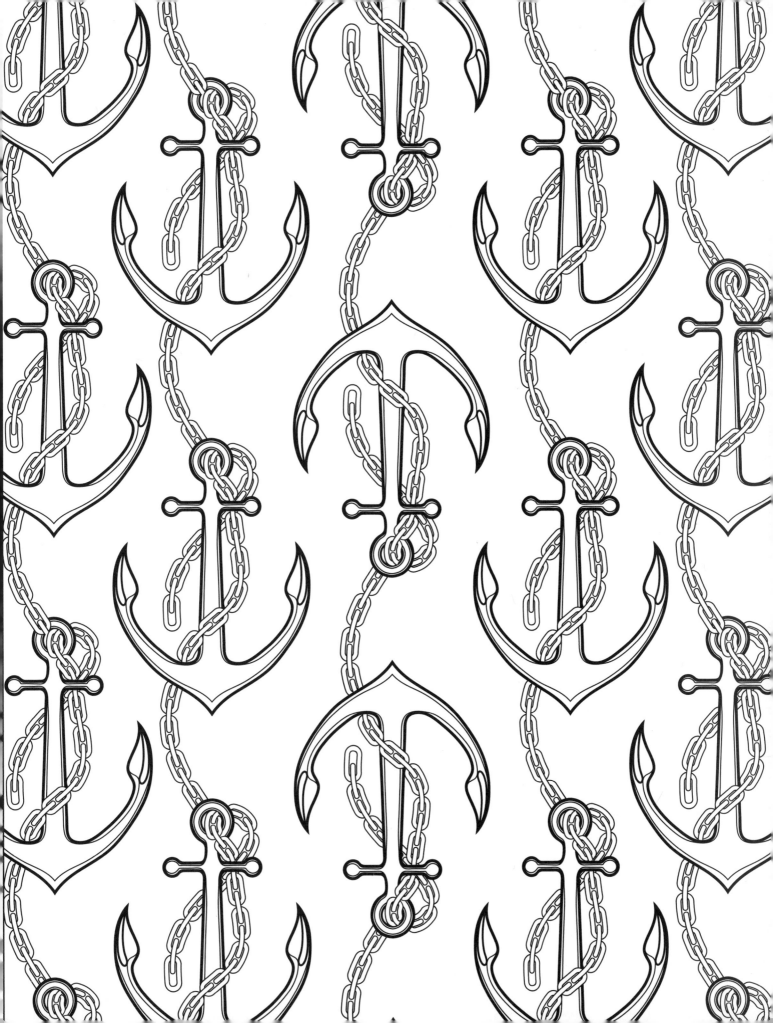

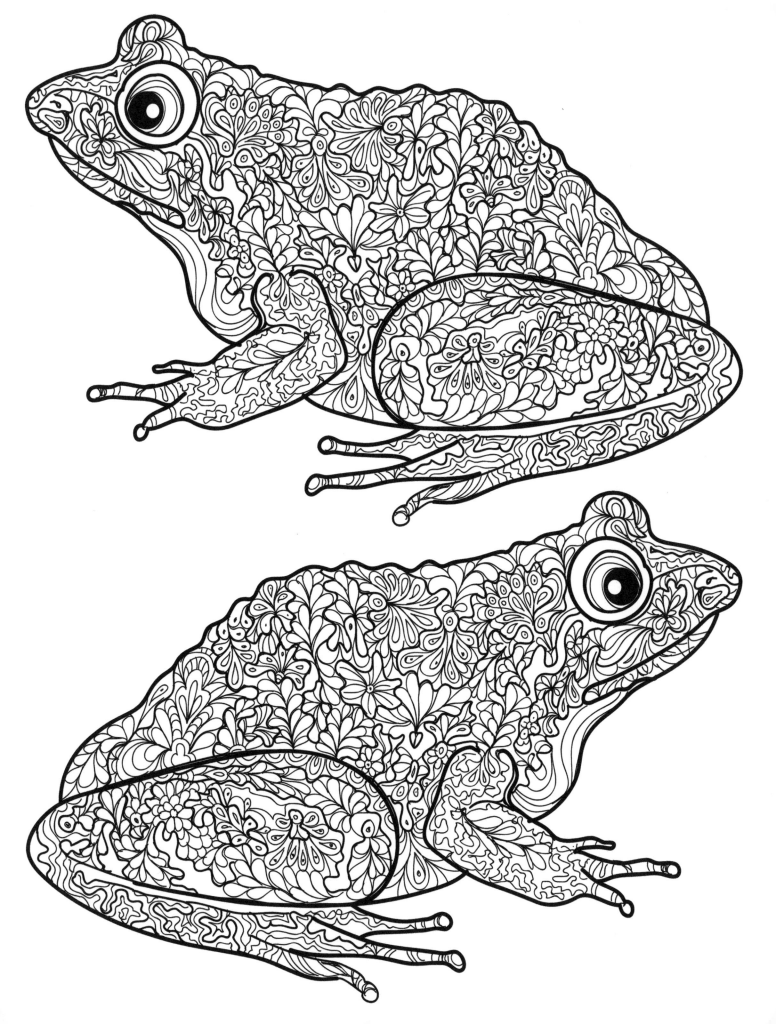

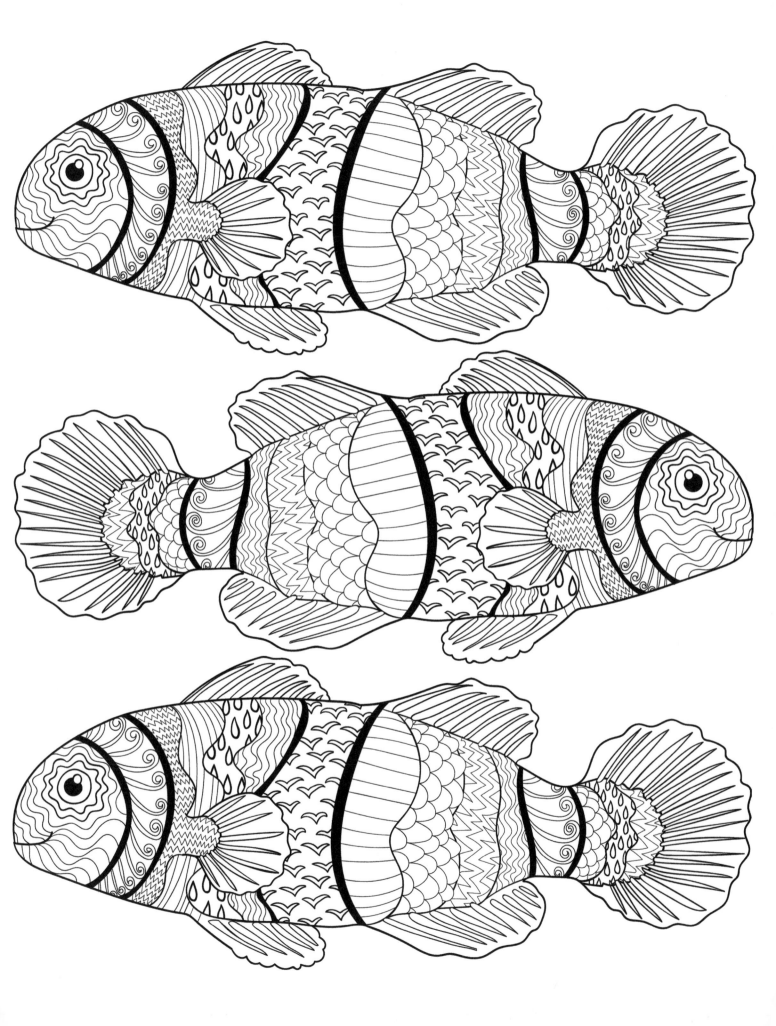

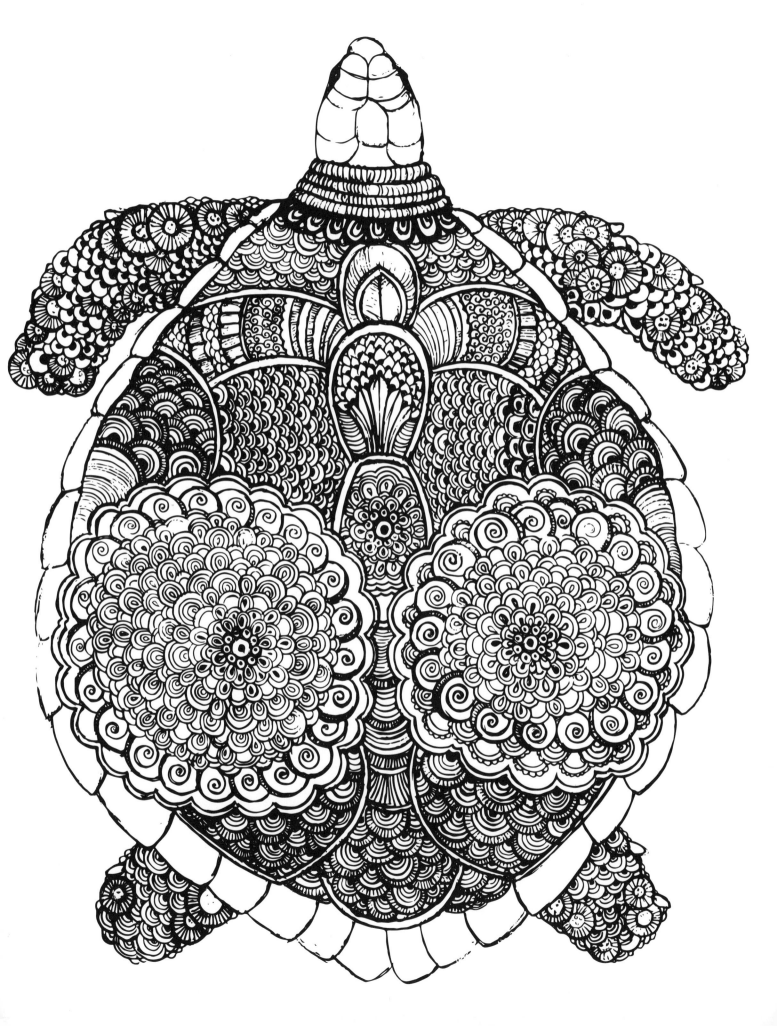

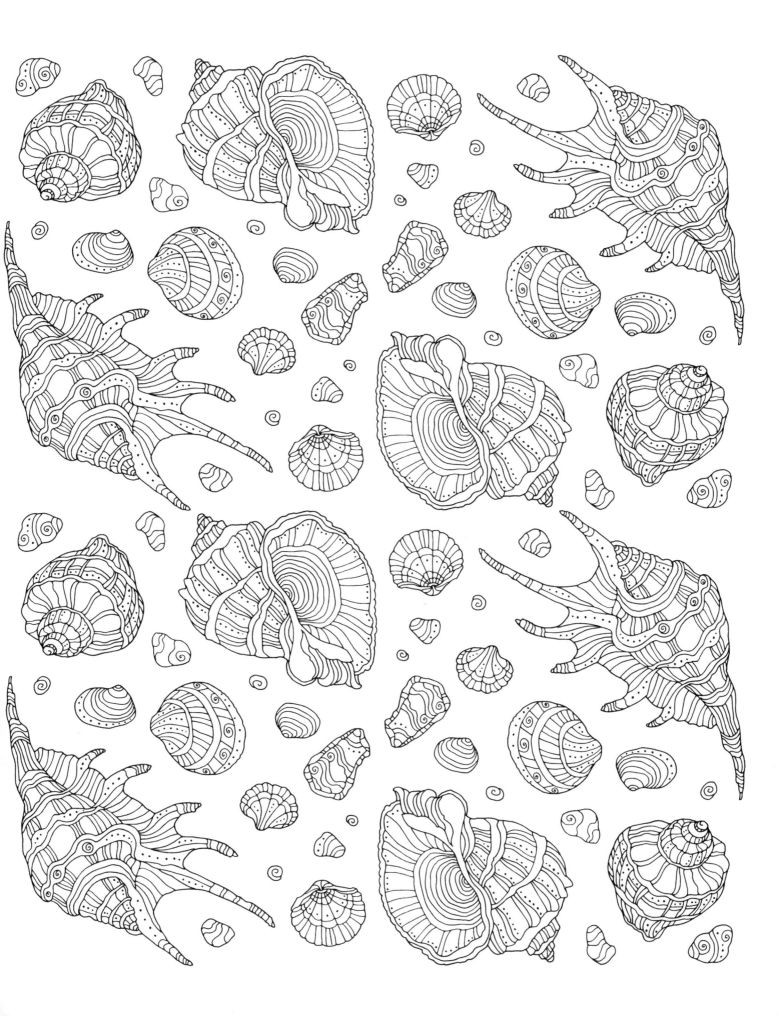

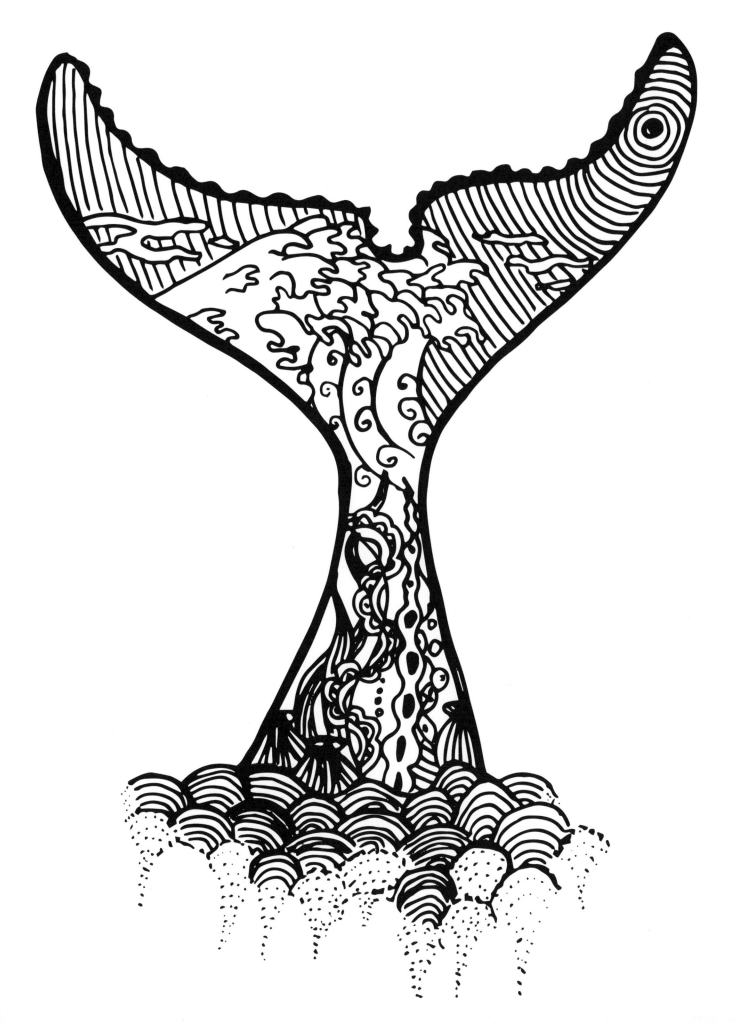

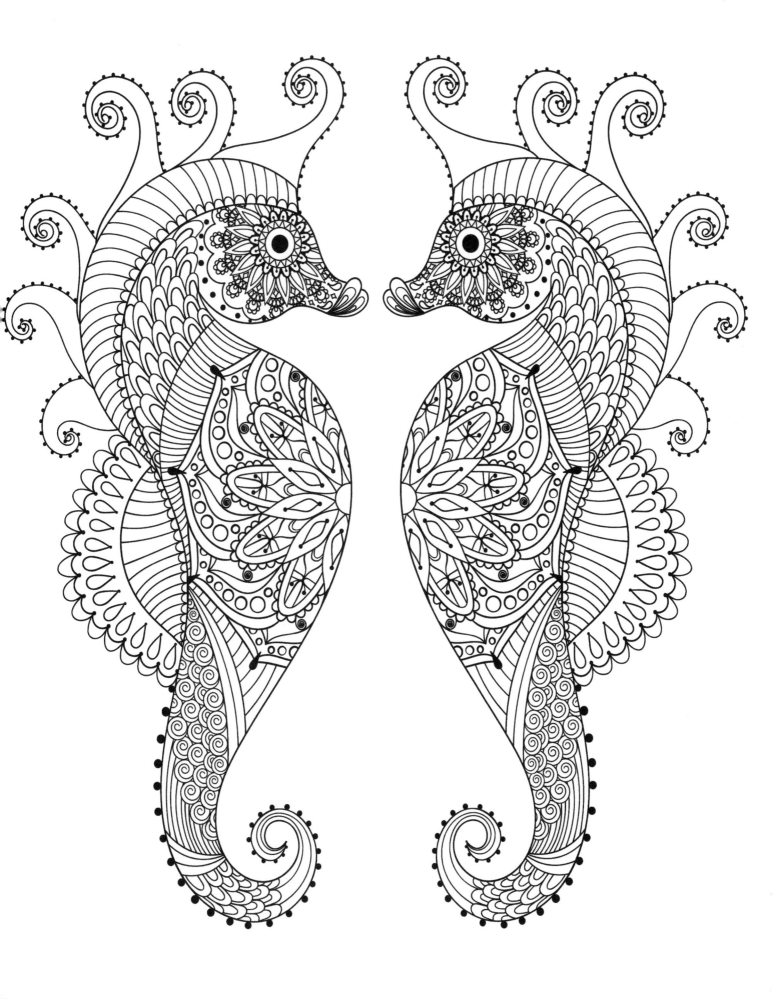

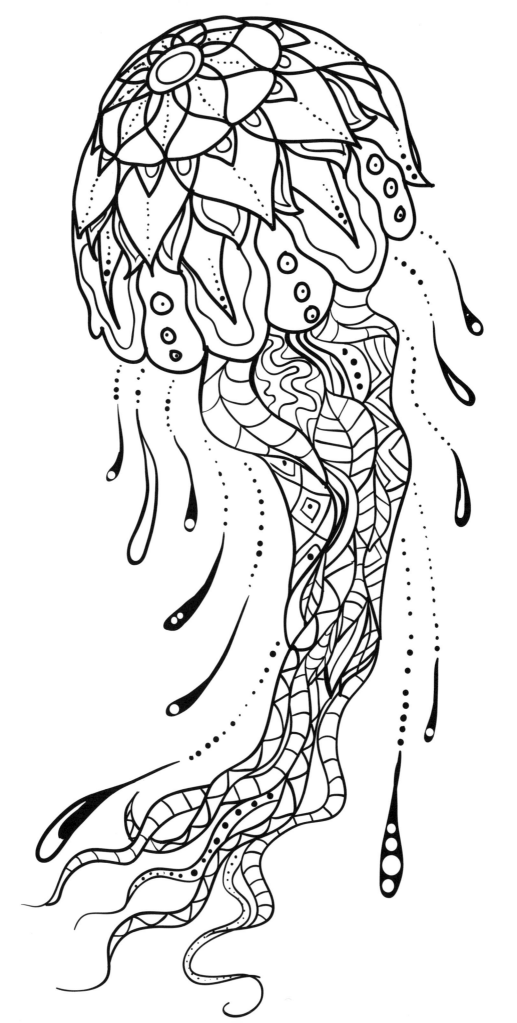

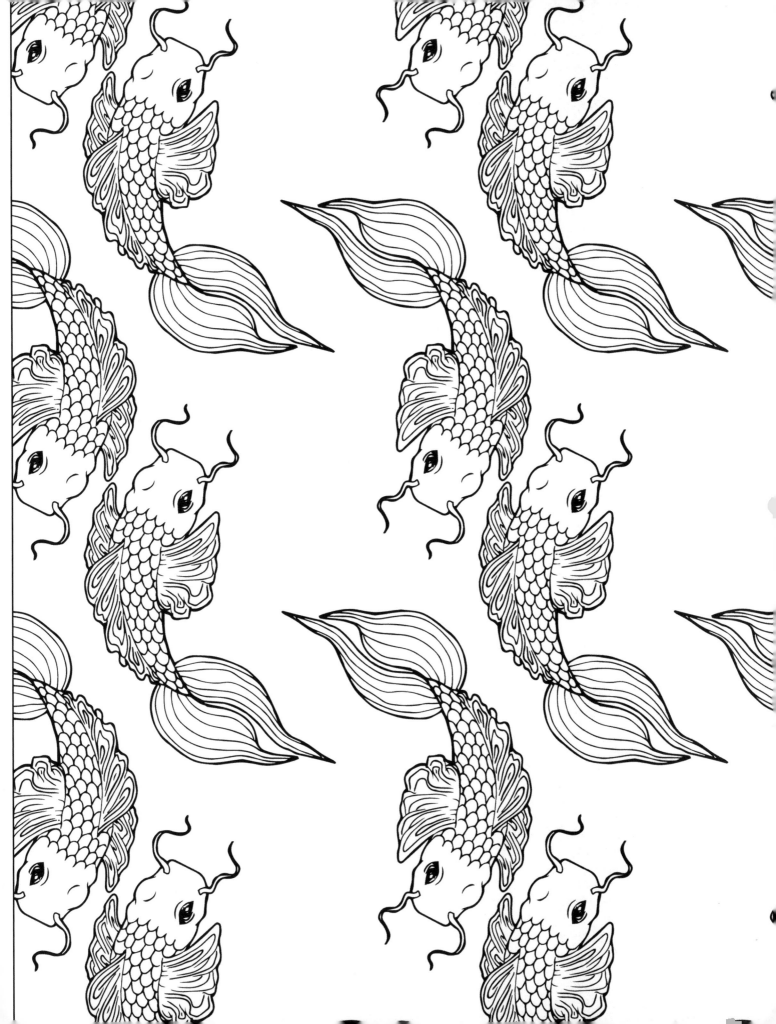

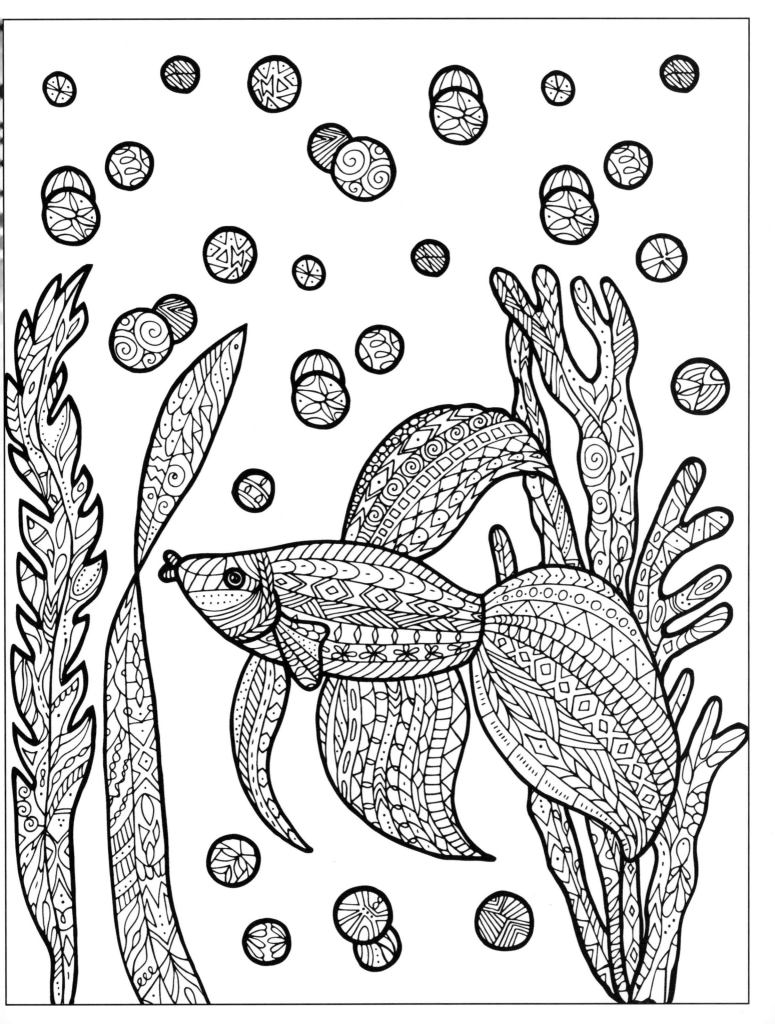

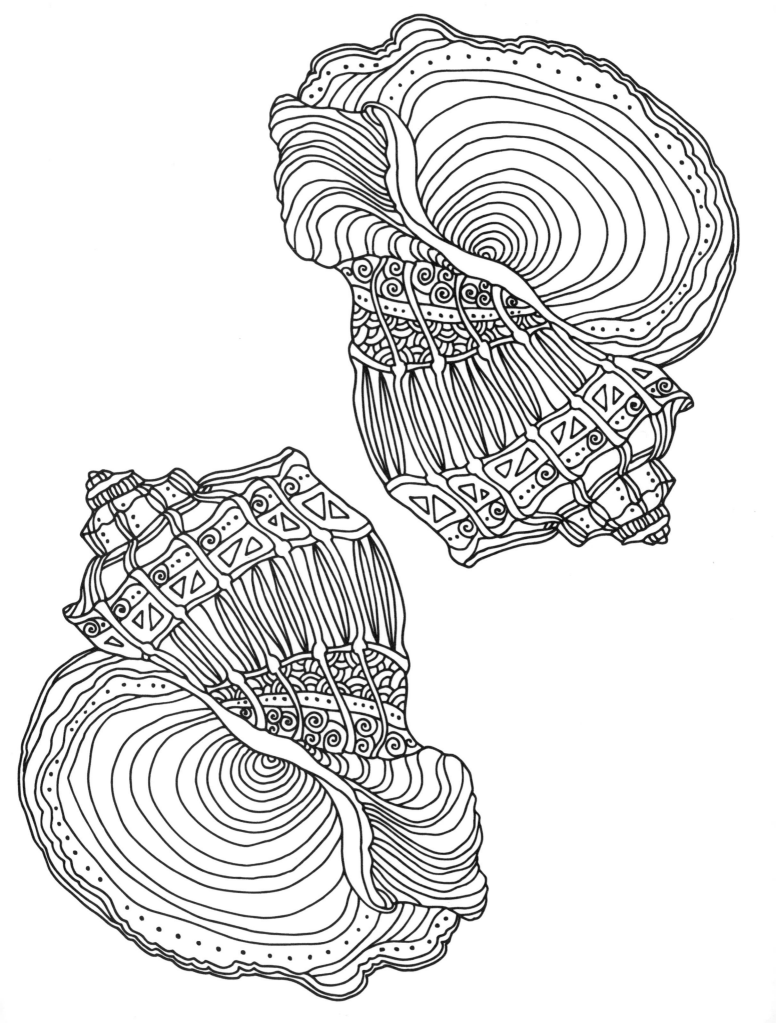

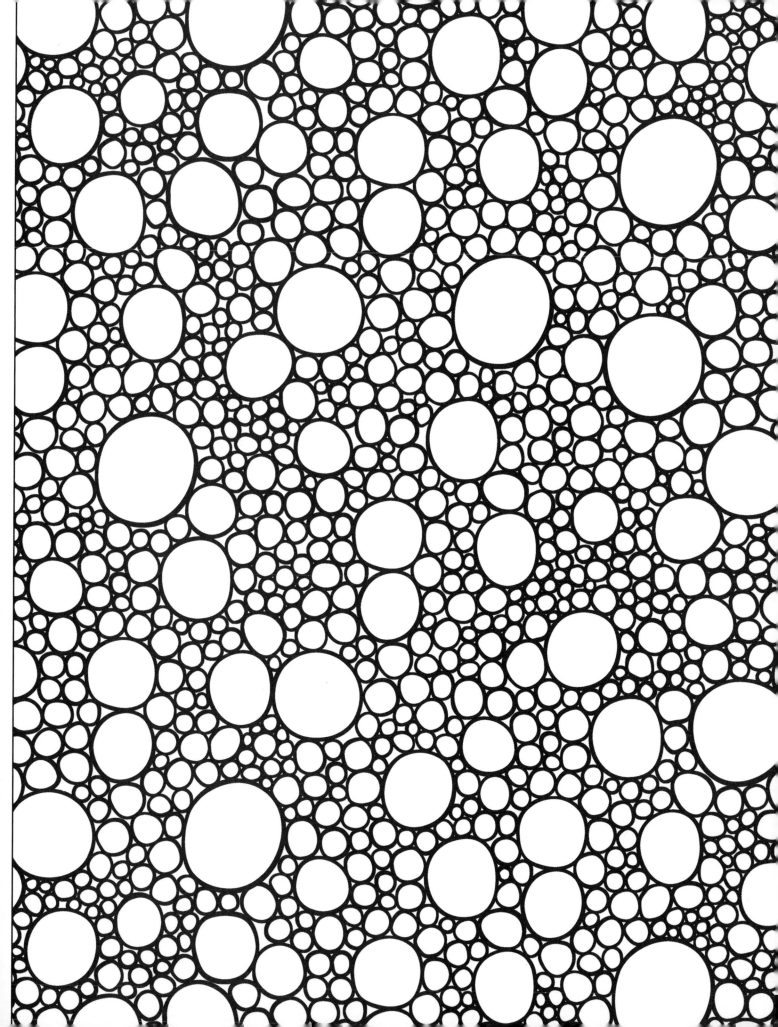

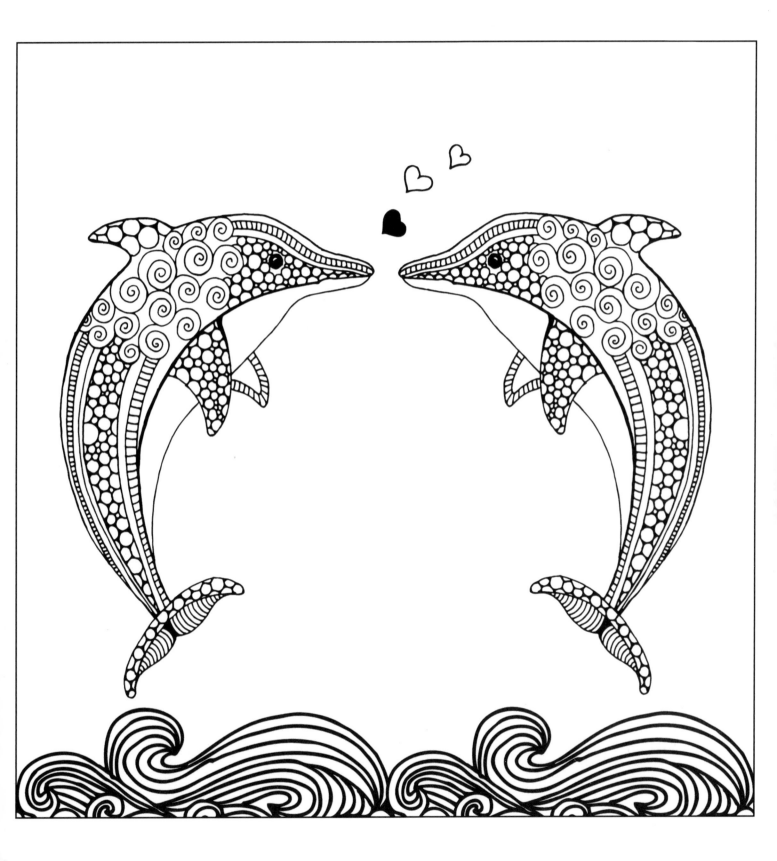

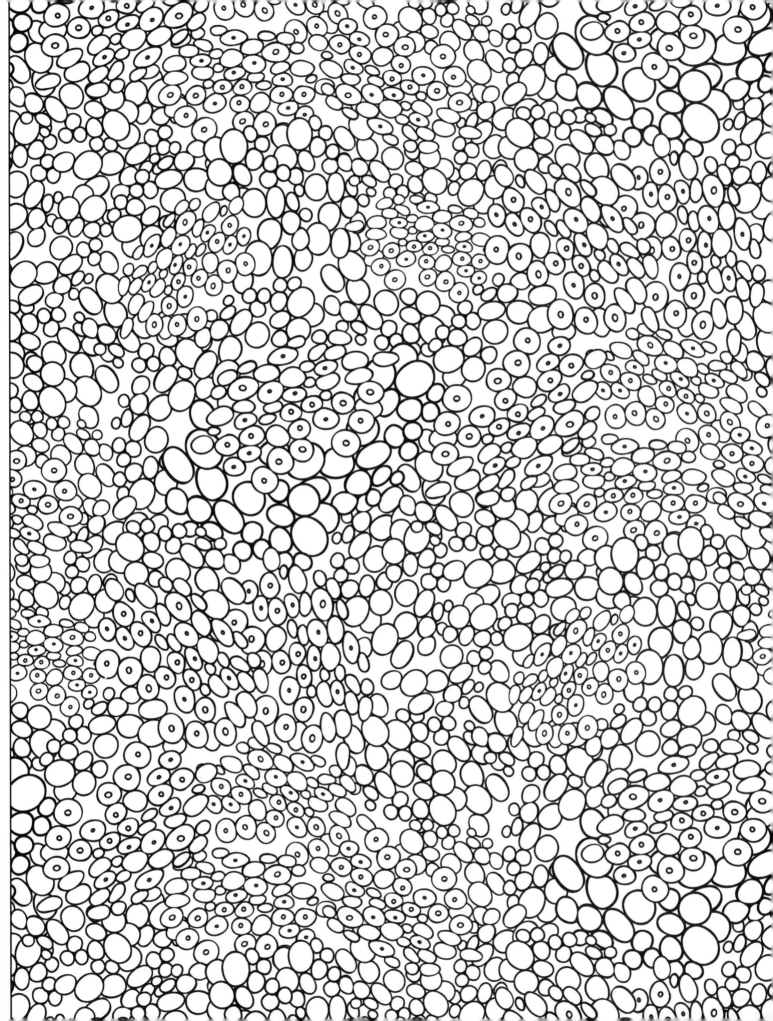

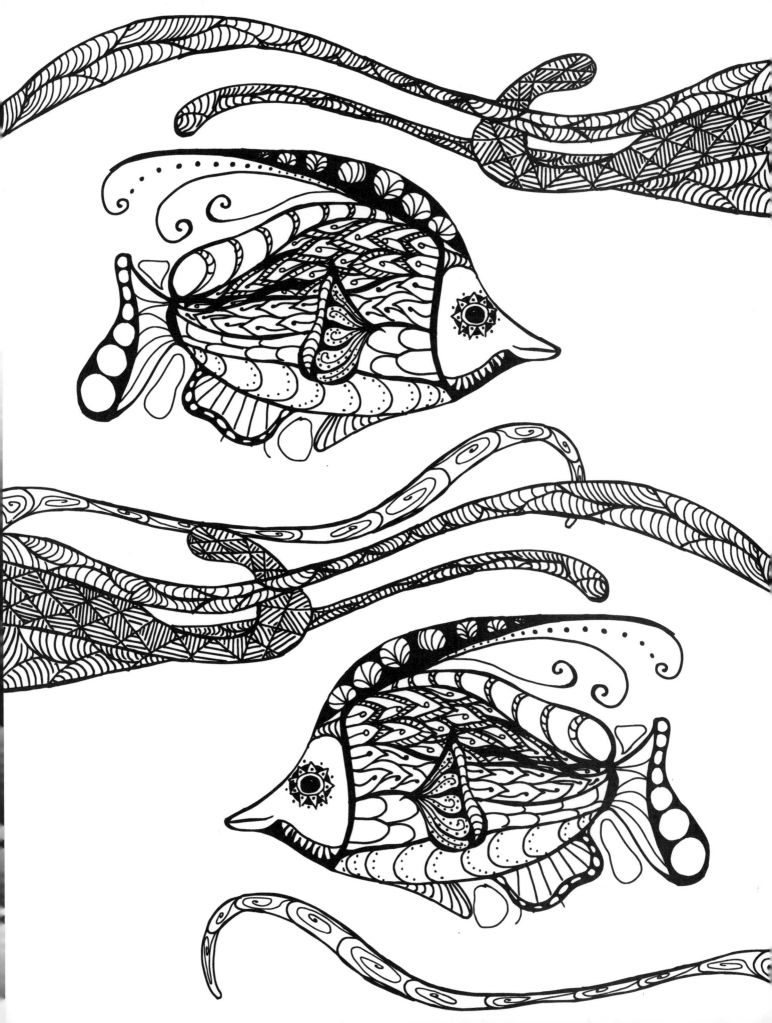